THE FABULOUS RADIO NBD

The Fabulous Radio NBD

Brandon Wentworth

Beech Hill Publishing Company
Southwest Harbor, Maine

Library of Congress Cataloging in Publication Data

Wentworth, Brandon, 1905–
　The fabulous Radio NBD.

　1. Radio NBD (Mount Desert Island, Me.)—History.
2. United States. Navy—Communication systems—History—
20th century. I. Title.
VG77.W46　1984　　　　359.9'83　　　　84-6439
ISBN 0-933786-07-7

© 1984 Brandon Wentworth

All rights reserved. No part of this work may be reproduced or used in any form or by any means—graphic, electronic, or mechanical, including photocopying devices, taping or information storage and retrieval systems—without written permission from the author.

Beech Hill Publishing Company
Southwest Harbor, Maine

Manufactured in the United States of America

Cover design and map by Dale Swensson

PREFACE

OF THE THOUSANDS of people who visit Acadia National Park each season, many enjoy the scenic Ocean Drive on Mount Desert Island. On this drive, after passing Otter Cliffs, one comes to a Park Service road sign which reads: *Fabbri Memorial*. A few yards beyond is the memorial itself, a large monument of red granite with a bronze plaque insert inscribed to the memory of Lieutenant Alessandro Fabbri.

Lieutenant Fabbri was awarded the coveted *Navy Cross* by President Woodrow Wilson at the end of World War I for creating what was considered to be the most important and the most efficient radio station in the world.

Herein is the story of how and why Lieutenant Fabbri conceived and developed this fabulous station as his patriotic contribution to the War effort. To my knowledge it is the only concise, most factually accurate, comprehensive, illustrated history ever published about the old Otter Cliffs Naval Radio Station NBD.

Much of my story deals with the actual experiences of the Navy radiomen who operated the station and leaders of the radio communications industry who built it. The story also goes into technical descriptions of the radio equipment and antenna systems the way they were from 1917 when America entered the War until several years after the Armistice. I hope to be forgiven for being carried away by some of the operator quotes about the old arc and spark transmitters. My interest in this antique radio gear stems from spending summers while attending Stanford University and for sometime after graduation as a professional wireless telegrapher aboard ships of the U.S. Merchant Marine. That was between 1924 and 1929. And it was during those years that I became intimately acquainted with shipboard versions of arc and spark transmitters. I operated both types, as one or the other was installed on the various vessels on which I served.

To lend further credence to the authenticity of this historical account, I can add that I've been a radio ham for over sixty years, from 1920 to the present. Also, I was a radio officer with the Army Air Corps throughout WW-II; and later an electronics engineer with the Federal Aviation Administration for twenty-two years until retirement. I'm now a year-round resident of Southwest Harbor, Maine.

The greatest reward to me from this story will be *recognition* by those who read it of the *Fabbri Memorial* and the old time top flight Navy radio operators and brilliant engineers who made it all possible.

HISTORIANS TELL US that the little town of Bar Harbor on Mount Desert Island, Maine, became popular about the turn of the century as a summer resort for the rich and enormously wealthy. Such financial giants as J.P. Morgan, Andrew Mellon and George Vanderbilt spent the summer time there in company with steel magnate Andrew Carnegie and other industrial tycoons of that golden age. They came to play and frolic, to escape the big city turmoil, to enjoy the Island's delightfully cool fresh air and to engage in a social whirl to eclipse all others. Extravagant parties were the vogue, staged at million dollar castle-like summer "cottages" and aboard palatial yachts. It is said that J.P. Morgan's sleek, black, 406′ steam yacht *Corsair* was a sight to behold, riding at anchor in the town's crowded harbor. The loveliest ladies of high society summered there too, including Mrs. John Jacob Astor, Barbara Hutton and Evelyn Walsh McLean who dazzled them all with her *Hope Diamond*.

Bar Harbor holds another claim to distinction, less glamorous perhaps, but vastly more rewarding to our nation's well-being. It was the site of "the most important and the most efficient 'radio' station in the world" — and here is how it all came about:

One other well-to-do socialite and yachtsman who spent the summers at Bar Harbor was a Mr. Alessandro Fabbri. He resided in a sumptuous shore front "cottage" on Eden Street, five miles north of Otter Cliffs, a high rocky promontory which juts boldly out into the Atlantic. Mr. Fabbri was not a playboy as were many of his contemporaries. Instead, he devoted much of his time to scientific endeavors, one of which was experimenting in wireless telegraphy. It became his principal hobby.

Sometime prior to WW-I, through knowledge he gained from studying the writings of one Hugo Gernsback and other authorities on the subject, plus invaluable assistance rendered by Mr. Ralph Tabbut, a prominent Bar Harbor radio amateur, circa 1912, Fabbri built himself a very elaborate wireless station. The transmitter, receiver and aerial system he constructed from a selection of coils, inductances, spark gaps, transformers, condensers, crystal detectors, switches, ear phones, wire, insulators and a

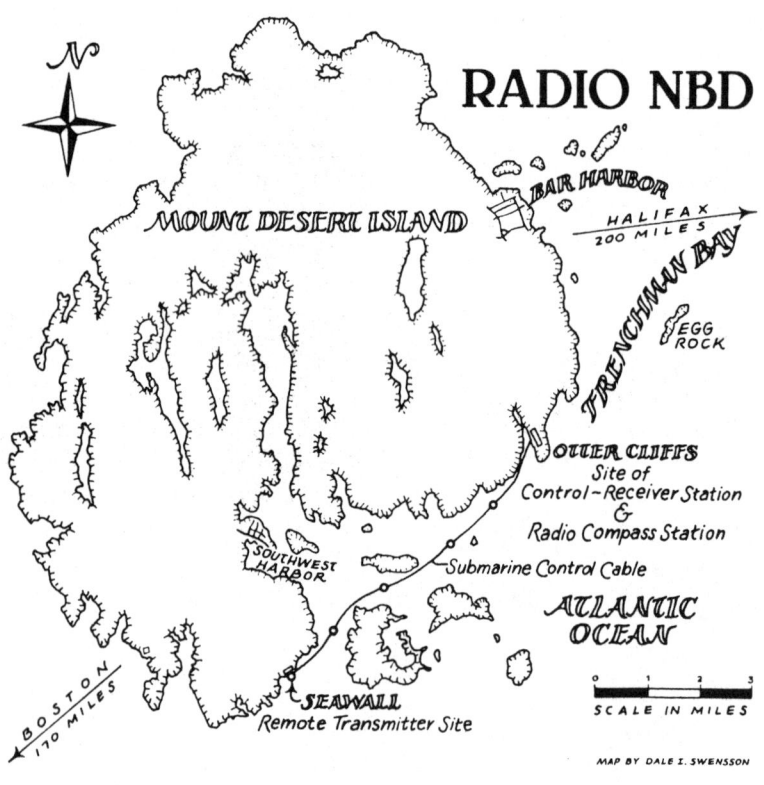

telegraph key purchased in New York and Boston. Mr. Tabbut helped him to put it all together and to string several long experimental antennas between tall spruce trees adjacent to his cottage. His ground system was the Atlantic Ocean.

To find out, among other things, how Mr. Fabbri learned the code I corresponded at some length with Ralph Tabbut. He replied, "On learning the code I do recall that he (Fabbri) and his brother Ernesto used a couple of buzzers and sent to each other for practice."

A word on Ernesto: Bar Harbor social registers have it that he was a partner in the House of Morgan, J.P.'s New York banking empire. His principal hobby was said to be yacht racing.

Ralph also told me that, "In those years there were only a few amateur, or ham stations around and distances between them were short. I recall that Fabbri, in striving for greater distances, began working ships at sea. One night when I was over at his house he worked an ocean liner headed for Europe. I don't remember the name of the passenger vessel, much less her call sign. That was certainly a long time ago wasn't it? In fact it was even before we had to have an amateur license!" Incidentally, when amateur licenses were first issued in 1912, Mr. Fabbri's was the tenth, with the call sign 1AJ.

Ralph's recollection of that ocean liner contact seems to reveal that Mr. Fabbri's interest in wireless communication may have stemmed from his many Atlantic crossings on what was said to be his favorite passenger ship, the North German Lloyd luxury liner *Kronprinzessin Cecilie*. Probably, as a fugitive from utter boredom, or business worries, he spent most of his time on the bridge chatting with Captain Charles Polack and his deck officers, or in the ship's radio room listening to incoming signals, conversing with wireless operator Simoni and watching him pound out the many messages. As a result, Mr. Fabbri apparently became quite well acquainted with Simoni who had been "sparks" on the *Cecilie* since her maiden voyage from Bremerhaven to Hoboken in 1907 and from whom Mr. Fabbri undoubtedly picked up much expertise in the art of professional wireless telegraphy.

On August 3rd, 1914 Great Britain declared war on Germany. The very next day, at the first break of dawn, the *Kron-*

North German Lloyd luxury liner *Kronprinzessin Cecilie* at anchor, Bar Harbor, Maine, August 4, 1914.
Photo courtesy Bar Harbor Historical Society.

prinzessin Cecilie came steaming into Frenchman Bay and dropped her anchors less than a half mile off shore from Mr. Fabbri's Bar Harbor cottage. She had taken refuge in neutral waters to escape the British battle cruiser *Essex* which had chased her half way across the Atlantic. The escape was heralded by newspapers at the time which reported that the *Kronprinzessin Cecilie* was on a voyage from New York to England with a cargo of $10,600,000 in gold bullion and $3,000,000 in silver bars. There were 1,216 passengers aboard (Fabbri was not among them). When two days out of Southampton her wireless operator intercepted an exchange of messages between a British warship and a French warship saying that the *Cecilie* was "close by" and that she was "The finest prize ever open to capture." This alarming intelligence plus a coded message reportedly received moments later from the vessel's owners in Bremerhaven, ordering her to return to New York, caused Captain Polack to turn his ship about immediately and run for it! She proceeded westward under forced draft. She ran totally blacked out at night, thru dense fog day and night at her maximum speed of over 24 knots. Passengers were said to be absolutely terrified as even the fog horn was silenced. To add to their fears, they were neither told, nor did they have the faintest suspicion where the ship was bound, until Mount Desert Island and then the Bar Harbor shore line loomed up through the early morning mists.

Why did Captain Polack choose tiny Bar Harbor as a haven of safety when the big ports of Portland, Boston and New York were on course, virtually dead ahead? Had he been warned of a blockade? Or, was it possibly because of his close acquaintance with Mr. Fabbri? In either case, one of his passengers was said to be C. Ledyard Blair, a wealthy New York broker and local yachtsman, who was able to pilot the big ship safely past Egg Rock, on up Frenchman Bay and into Bar Harbor. The passengers immediately disembarked and the gold bullion and silver were transported ashore by the revenue cutter *Androscoggin*.

Then, according to downeast chroniclers, the good people of Bar Harbor, including Mr. Fabbri, lavishly wined and dined Captain Polack and his officers during their forced sojourn in Frenchman Bay. It is reported that Mrs. Fabbri bought out the Star Theatre twice a week for the crew of the *Cecilie*. One may surmise that all hands were suitably entertained by such ancient thrillers as, *"The Clutching Hand"* or, *"The Perils of Pauline."*

Early one cold morning in November the *Kronprinzessin Cecilie* put to sea again, but under escort of two U.S. Navy destroyers. The proud vessel's next port o' call and what became of her afterward is another story, best told by Sandra Paretti in her historical novel, *The Magic Ship*.

Some two and a half years later, on April 6th, 1917, the United States of America declared war on Germany. Since Mr. Fabbri was beyond the gob or doughboy enlistment age, he decided he could best serve his country by donating both his yacht, the *Ajax*, and his wireless station to the Navy. He would upgrade the station consistent with the most advanced state of the art at his own expense.

The Navy was quick to accept the yacht, a Gloucester fisherman type hull, 125' overall, 23' beam, 14' draft and 200 tons displacement. She was rigged as a gaff-headed ketch and sported a diesel auxiliary engine. However, the wireless station offer encountered difficulties.

Mr Fabbri, to assure that his patriotic gift would be manned by experienced operators as efficient as the station he planned to build, and not by a bunch of "lids," or novices, asked that he be named station manager. He was advised by Navy brass in Washington that civilian management of such a communication facility in war time was strictly against Navy policy. If he wished to be placed in charge of the station he must at least achieve the rank of ensign in the Naval Reserve. That was understandable. Hence, Fabbri immediately applied for the required ensign's commission.

His application, in due time, was returned, marked DISAPPROVED, with no reasons whatsoever given for the rejection. The several special trips he made to Washington to try to find out *why* his application was turned down were to no avail. They got him exactly nowhere.

Evidently, Mr. Fabbri was a man of grim determination. Although bitterly discouraged, he didn't give up. In becoming a millionaire he discovered on many occasions that it is *who* you know rather than *what* you know that often turns the trick. So, as a last resort he called on an old friend and wealthy neighbor, a fellow yachtsman and summer resident of nearby Campobello Island, a gentleman named Franklin Delano Roosevelt, then Assistant Secretary of the Navy. The immediate action taken by Mr. Roosevelt promptly won Fabbri a commission as ensign in the United States Naval Reserve Force.

Then, about the end of May, he went up to the Wireless Specialty Apparatus Company in Boston and, with their chief engineer, Mr. J.A. Proctor, selected the most modern equipment available which included a 1 kw spark transmitter complete with quenched spark gap and Dubilier mica condensers.

Shortly thereafter, on June 12th, Mr. Proctor, in company with Navy Lieutenant Henry Gawler, went downeast to Bar Harbor. Gawler, as a civilian in peacetime, was the first U.S. radio inspector at District Office #1 in Boston, as established on July 1st, 1912 by act of Congress. It was Proctor who engineered the United Fruit Company's Tropical Radio Telegraph station WBF (originally, the station was installed atop Filene's department store in downtown Boston). These gentlemen, two of the most knowledgeable in their field, tested many locations for the new Bar Harbor radio station. They finally picked out a site on the Otter Cliffs promontory near the Otter Creek side which would be quite well shielded by spruce trees from any curious U-boats cruising off shore. As the site was leased by its owner to the Bar Harbor Country Club, Fabbri subleased it lock, stock and barrel for the Navy. The lease included a fine old club house which too became part of the Otter Cliffs radio station.

On May 29th, 1917 one of the first professional "brass pounders" arrived on the scene. He was Navy Radioman Herbert C. Hovenden. I am greatly indebted to Mr. Hovenden for much of the documentary material contained herein. Hovenden's first duty assignment was to staff the amateur radio station of Arthur Lawford which had been taken over by the Navy. It was located at 292 Main Street in downtown Bar Harbor. The station had a 1 kw transmitter with a rotary spark gap. Hovenden tells us:

The Bar Harbor Country Club building leased by Mr. Fabbri for use as NBD control and receiver station.   *Photo courtesy Carl Herr.*

"There were four operators who covered a 24-hour watch; Navy Radiomen J. Albert Stevens, Paul D. Sullivan, Chesleigh C. Chisholm and myself. The station neither received nor sent any messages for local (Navy) headquarters because we had a direct telegraph wire into the Boston Navy Yard. Our daily duty was to report to another amateur station (also Navy takeover) at Machias or Eastport, with a 'P O M S A T' which meant, 'Personnel-Operations-Material are functioning SATisfactorily.' They reported the same to us. We logged everything we heard but transmitted nothing except the above report. The call sign for Machias was AA3 and for Eastport AA4. Ours was AA2.

"One morning toward the end of August we heard a station calling Radio NAD, the Boston Navy Yard and using *our* call sign AA2! It turned out to be the new radio station down at Otter Cliffs. They were doing a little testing. We heard Boston report their signals as 'very strong'.

"On August 24, 1917, Washington assigned Navy Chief Raymond Cole to Bar Harbor to assure that all Navy legal and operational practices were observed at Otter Cliffs since he would be the only one there with long practical experience in Naval radio communications. Furthermore, Cole would be the only *regular* Navy man at the station—the rest would be Naval reservists (USNRF). He found the station nearly completed and all work progressing satisfactorily. The station was formally commissioned on August 28, 1917 at twelve noon sharp. The Bar Harbor station was simultaneously closed and the operating staff transferred to Otter Cliffs along with the call sign AA2, soon changed to K2B and eventually to NBD.

"During the commissioning ceremonies, conducted by Cole, Ensign Alessandro Fabbri stood by as the happiest of spectators. He then took over as 'officer-in-charge' and Chief Cole became his Executive Officer. Cole, commensurate with his greater responsibilities and the vital importance of the Otter Cliffs assignment, was advanced to the rank of 'Gunner' on September 24, 1917."

The Bar Harbor Historical Society Museum has in its archives copies of the old periodical *Acadian* in which there appears in serial form almost all of Mr. Fabbri's official correspondence with Washington. Several of his letters reveal the exasperating and highly discouraging runaround he endured at the hands of Washington bureaucrats in his determined fight to secure a lowly ensign's commission. He won it only when his good friend Franklin Roosevelt effectively came to his aid.

Some of his other letters tell of the early happenings at Otter Cliffs. In the interest of brevity I have paraphrased one of them as follows:

"The first of the new receiving equipment has begun to arrive. One item which the Navy sent us has been nicknamed by one of our operators as the 'audion on a shingle.' The term was coined in praise and not in any derogatory sense because this vacuum tube, a de Forest audion, and its oscillatory circuitry has given us our first capability of undamped (CW) signal reception. The first station heard was the powerful arc transmitter of Radio POZ in Nauen, Germany. Thus, we are now in the 'arc' reception mode of operation. To demonstrate, we telephoned the Wireless Specialty Apparatus Company in Boston the other day and asked them to listen carefully. We then placed a Baldwin mica diaphragm earphone on the mouthpiece of the telephone. Company personnel reported they could hear the signals from POZ eight feet from *their* telephone receiver!"

Mr. Hovenden has made available to me some of Raymond Cole's old personal records from which the following is quoted:

"By early 1918 we were copying news and other broadcasts from POZ and message traffic from station IDO in Italy and YN in Lyons, France. This latter station was sending five-letter code messages to us daily on a 24-hour basis. Our 1 kw spark transmitter was installed and ready for operation, but quiet most of the time; until December 7th, 1917 when Otter Cliffs received an urgent telephone call from the Boston Navy Yard asking that we try to contact Halifax, Nova Scotia. They had a report that an explosion had occurred there. We had strict instructions to use only the 'lead backed' four letter code book always at our left side— but, in this case, we were allowed to use the peace time Halifax call letters, VCS and to use plain English. This was because they didn't have our code. Boston had called VCS repeatedly and couldn't get an answer. We called once. They answered and said their antenna towers were almost demolished and they were us-

One of the trans-Atlantic long wave receiving positions, Otter Cliffs.
Photo courtesy Jesup Memorial Library.

ing auxilliary power. They then told us there had been a terrific explosion in the harbor which had leveled a good part of the city. We reported this to the Boston Navy Yard who immediately dispatched the hospital ship *U.S.S. Colony* with doctors, nurses and medical supplies to Halifax. Later, in contacting a sailor who was on another nearby ship by letter, he reported that this move was undoubtedly of tremendous help to the people of Halifax."

We recall what happened. The French munitions ship *Mont Blanc,* laden with 2,300 tons of picric acid and 3,000 tons of TNT was rammed by another vessel and blew up, right in the harbor. Half the city was left in ruins. Over 2,000 lost their lives.

To further paraphrase Fabbri's letters to Washington, he reports: "Our trans-Atlantic traffic is increasing and our Washington wire is kept very busy. Our daily 100% reception of YN in France throughout the 24 hours continues. My operators are doing a magnificent job especially when considering we are a receive-only station. Coded messages are sent to us each word *once*. Hence, the radioman on duty must 'get it' the first time or else! There is no opportunity for him to break-in for fills or repeats."

To shore up Otter Cliffs' transmission capability "just in case," the Navy replaced the 1 kw spark transmitter with a 5 kw set.

Fabbri had an older brother, Egisto. Not to be outdone by Alessandro he put up the money for construction of a tall lighthouse-shaped building to be located on the highest elevation of the Otter Cliffs peninsula. From the cupola of the structure one could enjoy a superb view of Frenchman Bay and the ocean beyond to the southeast. This lookout tower and a high barbwire fence around the station perimeter were Radio NBD's only security precautions against lurking enemy vessels and saboteurs.

In addition to information from Herbert Hovenden, Raymond Cole and Fabbri's letters, much herein was contributed by Frederick Grindle to whom I was referred by the curator of the Bar Harbor Historical Society Museum, Gladys O'Neil, as the gentleman who "knew all about" the old Otter Cliffs Naval Radio Station.

She was right. I found Mr. Grindle at his home in Bar Harbor. He told me he had served under Lt. Fabbri from the station's inception in 1917 until the end of 1921. He said he began as a telegraph operator at Otter Cliffs. Soon after he was promoted to "wire chief," in charge of the land line terminal in downtown Bar Harbor. It seems that all message traffic received by radio at Otter Cliffs was telegraphed via the terminal to Washington, by Morse wire. The return traffic to Radio YN in France was transmitted by the high power, long wave Naval radio stations NAA in Arlington (VA) and NFF in New Brunswick (NJ). Radio YN of course was the message traffic terminal for the American Expeditionary Forces in France.

Fred Grindle had another important responsibility at NBD. He was placed in charge of the very first high speed radio recording machine. The device was invented by a Dr. Hoxie of the General Electric Company. It was designed to record signals up to 1,000 words per minute. In Fred's words, "The recorder required some skill in making adjustments to the speed of the sender, adding tape while in operation and generally knowing how to keep it running smoothly. It worked like this: The incoming signal actuated a tiny mirror which reflected a light beam

Lookout tower, Otter Cliffs. After Armistice it became radio compass station. *Photo courtesy Carl Herr.*

Barbwire security fence, Otter Cliffs. Note telegraph pole line at right and antenna towers in distance. *Photo courtesy Carl Herr.*

"Gunner" Raymond Cole. Became full commander at end of W-II. Ray now resides in the San Francisco area.

Photo courtesy the Commander.

Herbert C. Hovenden on duty, Otter Cliffs, 1917.
Photo courtesy Mr. Hovenden

thru a tiny slit onto a moving sensitized paper tape. The tape was then run thru four long tubes; the developing tube, the fixer tube, the washer tube, the drying tube and then out. The tape was then read and translated by an operator from dots and dashes to numerals or letters on a typewriter. The operators were referred to as 'tape worms.' Although we made readable test tapes up to 900 WPM, we never actually recorded any incoming signals at over 45 to 50 WPM. You see, we had information that enemy submarines were transmitting their position and other reports at ultra high speeds—too fast for manual copy. But the U-boats we monitored were never able to attain any such speeds on their high power long wave transmitters, though if they ever did we were sure ready for 'em!"

Chief Petty Officer Frederick Grindle. As if WW-1 wasn't enough, Fred now fights the energy crunch at his home in Bar Harbor.
Photo courtesy Marion Varney.

Again from Fabbri's letters: "Night before last we intercepted a message from one European station to another on 4,000 meters. The suffix was, 'Please transmit this message to President Wilson since we have no direct means of radio communication.' We copied the message solid and had it in Washington within five minutes!" About mid-1918 Fabbri adds: "Handling over 20,000 words a day from Radio YN. A good percentage is in cypher. We are told that no other U.S. station is receiving YN on a solid day-to-day, around the clock basis."

With all that heavy traffic in coded and cypher messages coming in from YN, one can well imagine NBD was the key link in the "hot line" between President Woodrow Wilson and John "Blackjack" Pershing, Commanding General of the AEF. By early 1918 jamming loomed up as a serious problem. Oddly enough, the person to solve it was Dr. E.F.W. Alexanderson, the same

[15]

CPO Carl Herr at base of lookout tower, Otter Cliffs, 1919. Note he's out of uniform. He says it was his day off!

Photo courtesy of Mr. Herr.

genius who invented a transmitter powerful enough to jam every long wave receiver on earth. His solution is described in a letter, dated August 26, 1964 from Dr. H.H. Beverage to Herbert Hovenden. Here is the letter (in part):

> Dear Mr. Hovenden:
>
> Herewith are some notes relative to my activities at Otter Cliffs during World War I: Following a year as a testman at the General Electric Company, I was employed by Dr. E.F.W. Alexanderson in his radio laboratory in Schenectady and assisted in developing the long wave system based on the Alexanderson 200 kw alternator. My specialty was the development of a receiving system for the long waves.
>
> In 1917 there was concern that the Germans might cut all of the trans-Atlantic cables and jam reception of American radio stations in France, thereby cutting off all communications between Washington and the American Forces in France. The problem presented to Dr. Alexanderson was to devise a receiving system that

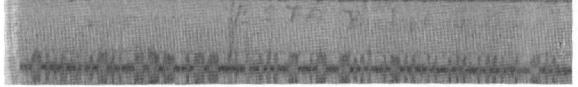

Radioman Adams at operating position for the Alexanderson Barrage Receiver (to his left). The high speed Hoxie Radio Recording Machine is at his right. Below is an actual sample of a recorded tape. The signal is from Radio POZ and includes the word "ESTABLISHED". Carl Herr has a notation on back of tape saying, "Apparently the POZ operator knew English!" *Photo and tape courtesy Mr. Herr.*

could be located in France with the capability of balancing out any jamming of the American stations by radiation from Germany. In addition, it was desired that the system should have two nulls* so that a transmitter could be erected somewhere in France to "barrage" jam the German receiving stations, without jamming our stations, thus preventing them from receiving the American radio signals. Hence the system was called the Barrage Receiver.

The Navy was greatly interested in both the anti-jamming and directional features of this antenna system and requested Dr. Alexanderson to have his Barrage Receiver installed at Otter Cliffs. I was the one to whom he assigned the job which as I recall went something like this:

During a rainy week at Otter Cliffs, I dragged rubber covered wires thru the woods and underbrush for two miles in opposite direc-

---

*A null is a characteristic of certain type antennas whereby minimum, or no signals at all, are received from a predetermined direction.

tions from the receiving station. The northeast wire terminated at Thunder Hole (a narrow cavern in the rocks exposed to the Atlantic's booming surf). The southwest wire extended to Hunter's Beach. As Lt. Fabbri expressed it, "The wires were draped from the mountain tops to the sea". The results were very good. The signals were considerably stronger and the static less on the barrage receiver than on the Pickard loop-vertical arrangement, already in use at Otter Cliffs.

Even without any balancing arrangement, the European signals were quite good on the northeast wire, while there was practically nothing but static on the southwest wire over the bridge across Otter Creek. Accordingly, I arranged to run a wire directly across the creek to a large tree on the far side. I had some difficulty in finding an able seaman who dared to climb the tree to hook on the wire, but it was finally accomplished. There was no improvement. The southwest wire still provided weak European signals and plenty of static. Finally, I took a receiver down to the southwest end of the southwest wire at Hunter's Beach and discovered that the European signals there were excellent and the static low, indicating that ground wires by themselves were substantially uni-directional. This led to the development of the Wave (Beverage) Antenna, the first *aperiodic* (uni-directional) antenna.

I received wonderful cooperation from everyone, especially from Lt. Fabbri and Ray Cole. I shall always recall with pleasure those days at Otter Cliffs where I met so many men that later were to contribute so much to the radio communication industry.

Sincerely yours,
/s/ H.H. Beverage

Frantic distress calls were also "jamming" Otter Cliffs. Again we quote from Mr. Hovenden: "On July 26, 1918 we started logging distress calls like, S O S - ALLO. ALLO meant 'sighted submarine.' Then would often follow the name of the ship and her position. This information was immediately wired to Washington. The enemy submarines were attacking our merchant shipping, starting off the coast of Florida and coming north. Navy Intelligence warned of their presence. An example advisory: 'Submarines operating as follows: July 19th off New York and in Lat. 41.15N - Long. 52.18 W. July 21st 10 miles NE Chatham, Mass. July 22nd Lat. 43.00 N - Long. 69.00 W.' etc.

"Here are a few distress calls from our log: July 27, 1918. 1:26PM. S O S 38.42 N 60.58 W. Speed 16 knots. Gunned and chased. 2:41PM. S O S de S/S *British Major* 39.58 N - 60.50 W. Course N50E true. Chased. 4:31PM. S O S *City of Bombay* 38.30 N - 65.45 W. Speed 13 knots. Gunned and chased. July 27th, 4 ALLOs. July 28th, 2 ALLOs, 1 S O S. July 30th, 2 ALLOs, 2 S O S. July 31, S/S *West Point,* chased, escaped.

"On August 1st Lieut. Cmdr. LeClair came up from Washington and said we were about the only shore station that was receiving these distress calls.

"On August 2nd Gunner Cole called all the men together and said, 'We are liable to wake up any morning and find ourselves half way to the moon as a result of a submarine attack!' Fortunately for all hands that never occurred."

Another note in Hovenden's diary: "October 1918. Inspection today by DCS. Says Otter Cliffs is doing better work than any other station in the U.S.A."

Mr. Hovenden continues: "From the almost constant steam of RUSH and RUSH—RUSH messages from our European station YN in France, we had concluded that an important message might be coming through at any time, although the 5-letter code which YN used disclosed nothing to our operators. But our conclusions were well warranted. In the early evening of October 6th, 1918, POZ opened up and called WSL for 15 or 20 minutes, with no reply. Radio POZ then broadcast the following:

PRESS 37 WDS 127-128 TRANSOCEAN PRESS NR. 2045 Fourth special sixth—The note transmitted to President Wilson through agency of Swiss government is as follows colon quote German government request President of United States of America to take his hand in restoration of peace comma to inform all beligerent states of this request and to invite them to send plenipotentiaries for the purpose of making negotiations stop It accepts programme presented by President of United States of America in message to Congress of Eight of January nineteen hundred eighteen and his later declarations comma especially address of twenty seventh of September as foundation for peace negotiations stop In order to prevent further bloodshed German government requests immediate conclusion of a general armstice on land water and in the air unquote stop.
   TRANSOCEAN BERLIN OCTOBER 6th 1918
      (8:58 PM)

According to Fred Grindle this is a true copy of the first German "surrender" message. Fred should know as he was there and has an original copy framed on the wall of his ham radio shack in Bar Harbor. It bears the endorsement, "Copied at Transatlantic Naval Radio Station, Otter Cliffs, Bar Harbor, Maine." He made a Xerox copy for me from which the above is transcribed. Incidentally, according to Fred, Germany had no alternate direct circuit routing for the message since the British Navy had cut all cables connecting the U.S. with Germany early in the War.

There is another rather ironic twist to this tale. It seems that German Telefunken interests built Radio WSL originally, at Sayville, Long Island (NY). About 1916 the station was taken over by the Navy. In 1918 a long wave 200 kw arc transmitter was installed and operated under the new call sign NDD. So, when the POZ operator called "WSL" with the first peace message that evening he was apparently unaware of this call sign change. His call book undoubtedly still listed the former Telefunken station as Radio WSL.

Mr. Grindle has another document framed on his wall. It is a citation addressed in large capital letters to FREDERICK GRINDLE. It spells out at great length all the many outstanding accomplishments of Radio NBD from August, 1917 thru December, 1923. It ends with the following:

"Such pioneering achievements were the result of hard work, exceptional skill, imagination, initiative and devotion to duty in keeping with the highest tradition of the Naval Service. Well done.

/s/ Rear Admiral Robert H. Weeks
Commander
Naval Communications Command
Washington, DC."

On one of my recent visits with Fred Grindle at his home in Bar Harbor we talked a little about his old friend Ralph Tabbut. Fred told me, "You know, Ralph and I were neighbors here. We lived in the same block when I was a kid. That was around

1912. When the War came along he tried to get into the Navy but was turned down. They discovered some physical disability. Too bad. He was really a great operator. He taught me a lot about wireless too, but I didn't get into it right then. Instead, I got my start in life as a Western Union messenger boy. I remember delivering hundreds of messages to the bridge of the big German four-stacker *Cecilie* while she was anchored down here in the harbor. That was way back in August, 1914. She came in here early one morning to escape an English warship, and I believe a French warship too, that had been chasing her. Golly, that *Cecilie*! She was sure a beautiful ship. I was aboard her many times delivering all those telegrams. She stayed here about three months as I recall." Then I asked, "By the way Fred, who do you suppose was the Captain's Bar Harbor friend who decided him to put in here that morning?" He replied without a moment's hesitation, "Fabbri."

With all the sophisticated antennas installed at Otter Cliffs, including the "barrage receiver" Beverage and several 30' high by 90' long vertical loops, plus the efficient receivers which these antennas served, that 5 kw spark set was like the proverbial bull in a china closet. A spark transmitter of that magnitude, if operated in the midst of highly sensitive receivers, would completely jam any and all incoming signals, no matter how strong. Gunner Cole decided well before the Armistice they'd better do something about it. So, he selected an area at the southern end of the Island, between the ocean and a salt water swamp, at a place called Seawall, some six air miles southwest of Otter Cliffs. Here the Navy built a remote transmitter site.

The antenna was a 400' flat top supported by two 220' guyed, wooden lattice-work towers. The ground system consisted of a 20' square heavy copper wire grid extending some 225' beyond each tower. All wires were bonded and those on the southeast side extended into the ocean. A two story building was constructed to house the equipment which included a newly acquired arc transmitter, two motor generators and the 5 kw spark set. The transmitters were controlled from Otter Cliffs thru a submarine cable. Both the arc and spark transmitters were placed in full

Lieutenant Alessandro Fabbri

Photo courtesy Frederick Grindle.

The remote transmitter site at Seawall. According to Fred Grindle, the intrepid motor bike rider is none other than his old friend Carl Herr.
Photo courtesy Mr. Grindle.

operation immediately after the Armistice. According to Gunner Cole, the range of each transmitter was "most remarkable."

After the Armistice, NBD's message traffic instead of slowing down accelerated rapidly. On January 25th, 1919, Gunner Cole was transferred to sea duty as Radio Material Officer on the big German vessel *Vaterland,* taken over by our Navy and renamed *Leviathan.* In one of his letters he wrote: "We called Otter Cliffs to make sure the 'regulars' were available. They were there, ready and standing by. We then sent 1080 messages in less than 24 hours. I batted out over 250 of them myself. On that one trip to New York the *Leviathan* carried 17,000 returning troops!"

Again on March 31, 1919, Fabbri reported: "In two hours we have taken nearly 200 commercial messages from the *Leviathan* when she was 1,000 miles out of New York." He adds: "Most inbound ships clear their traffic through Otter Cliffs where reception is usually better than at other stations along the coast." By

The operating position for the arc and spark transmitters, Otter Cliffs.
Photo courtesy Jesup Memorial Library.

U.S. Navy seaplane NC-4, with WW-I destroyer below.
Photo courtesy Carl Herr.

then, Fabbri had been promoted to a lieutenant in the U.S.N.R.F.

May 8 to 31, 1919, witnessed the first successful west-east trans-Atlantic airplane flight. It was made by U.S. Navy Lieut. Cmdr. Albert C. Read and crew from Rockaway, Long Island to Plymouth, England in the seaplane NC-4; flying time 52 hrs, 31 mins. On May 17th, according to Fabbri, Radio NBD was in continuous direct two-way communication with NC-4 cruising at 10,000' on the leg between Trepassey Bay, Newfoundland and Horta in the Azores, a distance of some 1,000 nautical miles. The aircraft was equipped with a ½ kw spark set. Radio operator aboard was Ensign Herbert Rodd. Mr. Roosevelt sent a congratulatory message to pilot Read and crew via Otter Cliffs. An acknowledgement was back in Washington in three minutes, according to Fabbri.

The latter part of June, 1919 found President Wilson enroute Europe on the *U.S.S. George Washington* to sign the peace treaty. According to Mr. Hovenden, Otter Cliffs, using the remoted arc and spark transmitters at Seawall, handled a large number of messages for the President and his staff. On his return voyage the President authorized the skipper of the *George Washington* to prepare a letter of commendation, the text of which is quoted as follows:

> During the voyage of this vessel, carrying the President from Brest, France to Hoboken, New Jersey, a tremendous amount of message traffic was handled by Navy Radio, Bar Harbor, Maine. The operators on duty showed a perfect knowledge of regulations and their efficient operating was a great help in rapidly clearing the President's traffic.
>
> /s/ Woodrow Wilson
> By: Direction
>
> E. McCauley
> Rear Admiral USN

The letter was sent to Charles B. Ellsworth, Chief Radioman, NBD.

The chief radioman on the *George Washington* was said to be Fred Schnell who later became prominent as traffic manager for the American Radio Relay League. On May 28th, 1919, Fabbri wrote a letter to Lieut. Cmdr. A. Hoyt Taylor in Washington.

Lieutenant Fabbri with his officers and crew, Otter Cliffs, March 27, 1919. *Photo courtesy Herbert C. Hovenden.*

The Pickard directional loop receiving antenna, Otter Cliffs.
Photo courtesy Jesup Memorial Library.

At that time Commander Taylor was the Navy's Trans-Atlantic Communications Officer. The letter read: "Trans-Atlantic reception has been very satisfactory for the past many months. We have received as high as 28,000 words in one day — words *once,* without repeat. Our best record of traffic is 54,000 words in 48 hours, including 1,003 messages from ships, Government and commercial. As you know, Radio NSS at Annapolis with their new high power 500 kw arc installation is now our principal American transmitting station for European traffic." A few months later, according to Fabbri, the traffic totals had risen to several times that figure and the station had grown to a complement of 170/180 men, excluding officers.

Again we quote from Mr. Hovenden: "Otter Cliffs became the Navy's principal receiving station for trans-Atlantic messages. Ingenius systems of directional loop antennas, counterpoises and submarine ground wires were added; each serving a separate receiver installed in a separate building. Each receiver was for a specific European station — some transmitting on a definite schedule. Messages continued to be forwarded to Washington, New York and other addressees by land line telegraph."

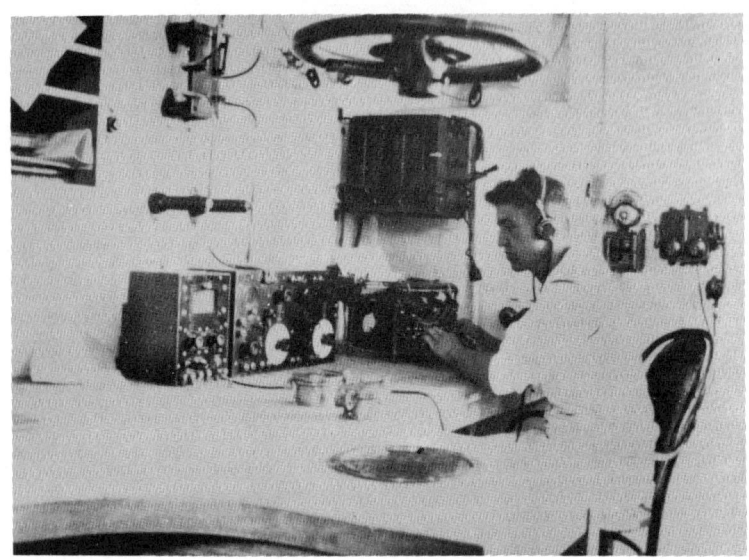

Long wave receiving position, Otter Cliffs. Radioman unidentified. Wheel above his head is for orientation of the Pickard directional loop antenna. *Photo courtesy Carl Herr.*

Here is a confirming quote from a Navy Department historical publication of 1922: "After Otter Cliffs had been properly equipped and new circuits installed, the copy made at that station was so certain that the Belmar (NJ) receiving station was, in February, 1919, closed and returned to the Marconi Company. Combined with the advantages due to the geographical location of Bar Harbor, the station there was amply able to care for trans-Atlantic copy."

In sifting thru the voluminous amount of reference material for this narrative, I came across several conflicting reports on the power rating of Radio NBD's arc transmitter. So, to set my record straight, I called on Ted Hancock of Southwest Harbor, a village three miles north of Seawall. Mr. Hancock was a Navy radioman assigned to duty at the Seawall remote transmitter site from 1923 to 1925. He told me the arc was a 12 kw transmitter. To prove it, he picked up a pair of scissors and cut a *captioned* picture of the rig out of his old photograph album and graciously handed it to me with, "Here, you keep it." Of course I thanked him pro-

[28]

fusely and then asked Mr. Hancock what duties he remembered best about Seawall. He replied more or less as follows: "Well, I still recall several. One was to make sure the drip cup above the arc electrodes was kept filled with alcohol and that the drip rate was proper. That arc in order to generate low frequency radio waves had to burn within an airtight enclosure in an atmosphere of hydrogen. The arc made its own hydrogen from the alcohol dripping on it. It reminds me of the magazine advertisement which shows Jack Daniel's whiskey being charcoal mellowed, drop by drop. Same idea. Also, it was my job to switch the big antenna from the arc to the spark transmitter when ordered to do so by the control station at Otter Cliffs. Speaking of that spark set, every once in a while the clear, bell-like 500 cycle note would go sour because of a leaky mica gasket between two of the thirty or so quenched gap elements. Then I'd have to change them all to clear up the note. But what I'll never forget for the rest of my days is the standby power plant. It was an old diesel one-lunger with a flywheel as big as your house. To start her, I'd climb up and heat the firing pin red hot with my blowtorch. Then I'd jump down fast and turn on the compressed air—and away she went!"

Following the Armistice, the lookout tower near the brink of Otter Cliffs was converted to a Radio Compass station. Chief Carl Herr was the CPO in charge. Among many other "saves", Herr reports that his compass facility once helped prevent the British cruiser *Raleigh* from running head-on into Egg Rock—a small islet—when entering Frenchman Bay in dense fog. He states, "The *Raleigh* backed down—engines full astern—thus avoided going aground, by a timely bearing and warning from our compass station. The *Raleigh* sent a British major out to Otter Cliffs the next day to explain this happening and to thank us."

Chief Herr tells of another timely rescue: "On July 2nd, 1919, we intercepted an S O S from the British dirigible *R-34*. This was the first crossing of the Atlantic Ocean by an airship. She reported they were running low on fuel because of strong head winds and might not be able to reach their destination—Mineola, N.Y. One of the Navy's destroyers dispatched to her estimated position, confirmed by bearings from our radio compass, advised

The 12 kw arc transmitter at Seawall. Note alcohol drip cup at top.

Photo courtesy Ted Hancock.

the airship to descend to a lower altitude where they would probably encounter less wind. They did this. Otter Cliffs then kept the airship advised of weather conditions on the remaining route until she reached her destination safely. The Commanding Officer of the dirigible was so grateful that he asked Otter Cliffs to handle all weather information during *R-34*'s return flight to Scotland."

On Armistice Day, November 11, 1920, the President of the United States awarded Lieutenant Fabbri the coveted NAVY CROSS. The citation which accompanied this high award reads as follows:

Ted Hancock's pride and joy. The standby power plant at Seawall.
Photo courtesy Carl Herr.

The Radio Compass operating position in the lookout tower, Otter Cliffs. The wheel is to zero in a directional loop antenna (in cupola above) on the bearing of an incoming signal.

Photo courtesy Carl Herr.

   For exceptionally meritorious service in a duty of great responsibility in the development of the radio receiving station at Otter Cliffs, Maine, and the small receiving station at Seawall. Under Lt. Fabbri's direction the station was developed from a small amateur experimental station until, at the end of the War, it was the most important and the most efficient station in the world.

> . For the President
> /s/ Josephus Daniels
> Secretary of the Navy

   The Navy Cross itself, with its little blue and white ribbon, is in the Bar Harbor Historical Society Museum together with the citation, a large portrait photograph of Fabbri, and his elegant "dress parade" Navy sword.
   On January 23rd, 1921, Fabbri wrote the following letter to Alfred J. Ball, the radio operator on duty at Otter Cliffs who, on November 10, 1918, copied Germany's fourth and final peace message direct from Radio POZ:

[32]

In case you do not already know it, I'm sure you will be glad to learn that the station was awarded the Navy Cross for its services during the War. As Commanding Officer, I was the recipient of the decoration—but you and the others, on whom I chiefly relied, may well feel that you each own a share in this honor. I am enclosing a clipping from the Bar Harbor Times which shows you the citation.

This same clipping from the Bar Harbor Times goes on to report: "The decoration was received by Lieut. Fabbri at his home here. It was characteristic of the gentleman that, when some of his friends called to congratulate him, his comment was: 'I deserve but one two-hundredth part of the honor. The officers and men who served with me deserve as much of the credit as I do."

On February 6th, 1922, at the age of only 44, Fabbri crossed the bar for the last time. He died of pneumonia contracted on a hunting trip. He had resigned his Navy commission and was retired.

In 1935, except for the radio compass facility, all the Navy installations at Otter Cliffs and Seawall were razed. They had far outlived their usefulness. Through the intervention of John D. Rockefeller Jr., of nearby Seal Harbor, the radio compass, later known as a Radio Direction Finder (RDF) facility was moved across Frenchman Bay to Moose Island at the tip of Schoodic Peninsula in order that Otter Cliffs could become part of our National Park System. Rockefeller interests were also instrumental, fund-wise, in the building of a scenic road around the periphery of Otter Cliffs Point. Along this road, just across from where the old Otter Cliffs receiving station stood, the Bar Harbor townspeople got together and in 1939 erected a monument, a big boulder of the Island's red granite, with bronze plaque appropriately inscribed, as a memorial to *their* Lieut. Fabbri.

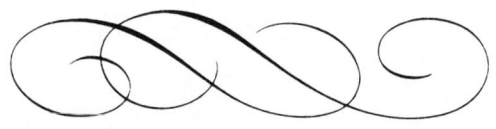

The Fabbri Memorial Monument, Otter Cliffs. National Park Service ranger is the well-known radio amateur Bill Townsend of Bar Harbor.
Photo by author.

Today, Otter Cliffs are within the boundaries of the Acadia National Park for all our people to visit and enjoy, even rock climbers who assault the face of those precipice walls in a risky attempt to defy the laws of gravity. Seawall too is part of Acadia National Park. It is a massive granite ledge where hungry herring gulls perch by the hour patiently awaiting a handout from the affluent summer visitor. Except for his memorial monument, framed by a semi circle of tall spruce trees, Lieutenant Alessandro Fabbri's Radio NBD is long gone from Mount Desert Island.